INSIDE THE NHL

Philadelphia Flyers

Claryssa Lozano

www.av2books.com

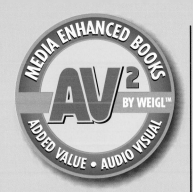

AV² provides enriched content that supplements and complements this book. Weigl's AV² books strive to create inspired learning and engage young minds in a total learning experience.

Your AV² Media Enhanced books come alive with...

Audio
Listen to sections of the book read aloud.

Key Words
Study vocabulary, and complete a matching word activity.

Go to **www.av2books.com**, and enter this book's unique code.

Video
Watch informative video clips.

Quizzes
Test your knowledge.

BOOK CODE

Y 2 6 7 3 5 9

Embedded Weblinks
Gain additional information for research.

Slide Show
View images and captions, and prepare a presentation.

AV² by Weigl brings you media enhanced books that support active learning.

Try This!
Complete activities and hands-on experiments.

... and much, much more!

Published by AV² by Weigl
350 5th Avenue, 59th Floor
New York, NY 10118
Websites: www.av2books.com   www.weigl.com

Library of Congress Control Number: 2014951870

ISBN 978-1-4896-3170-1 (hardcover)
ISBN 978-1-4896-3171-8 (single-user eBook)
ISBN 978-1-4896-3172-5 (multi-user eBook)

Printed in the United States of America in Brainerd, Minnesota
1 2 3 4 5 6 7 8 9 0   19 18 17 16 15

032015
WEP050315

Senior Editor Heather Kissock
Art Director Terry Paulhus

Photo Credits
Every reasonable effort has been made to trace ownership and to obtain permission to reprint copyright material. The publishers would be pleased to have any errors or omissions brought to their attention so that they may be corrected in subsequent printings.

Weigl acknowledges Getty Images and iStock as its primary image suppliers for this title.

Philadelphia Flyers

CONTENTS

Introduction

The Philadelphia Flyers opened play as a National Hockey League (NHL) **franchise** when the league first expanded in 1967. In that very first season, they reached the **playoffs**, setting a trend for many winning seasons to follow. The Flyers were as tough as their home city. Their very competitive nature, and address on Broad Street in Philadelphia, earned them the nickname, the Broad Street Bullies. The Flyers bullied their way to back-to-back Stanley Cups in 1974 and 1975. The team has appeared in the finals six more times since then.

In 2012 and again in 2014, Claude Giroux finished third in the league in scoring.

Although they have not hoisted the Cup in 40 years, the Flyers are ranked second in the NHL with an overall win percentage of 57.7. For the past 20 seasons, the Flyers have only missed the playoffs once. With a solid core of players, veteran leadership, and rising stars, the Flyers are poised to kick that championship door open once again.

Craig Berube played in the NHL for 17 seasons, 14 of them with the Flyers. He is currently the Flyers' head coach.

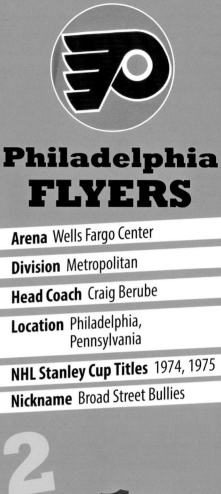

Philadelphia
FLYERS

Arena Wells Fargo Center

Division Metropolitan

Head Coach Craig Berube

Location Philadelphia, Pennsylvania

NHL Stanley Cup Titles 1974, 1975

Nickname Broad Street Bullies

2 Stanley Cup wins

16 Division Championships

8 Conference Championships

37 Playoff appearances

History

Lou Angotti was the first captain of the Flyers. Though he only played with the Flyers for one year in 1967–1968, he led the team with 49 points.

Ed Snider had the bright idea to bring professional hockey to Philadelphia in the early 1960s. In order to cover the $2 million **expansion** fee, Snider teamed up with investors Bill Putnam and Joe Scott. On December 9, 1966, their efforts paid off and the NHL awarded Philadelphia a franchise. The team's first arena was built shortly thereafter. The Flyers played their first home game on October 19, 1967, defeating their would-be crosstown rivals, the Pittsburgh Penguins, in a 1-0 **shutout**. Their first home win was an indicator of years of success to follow.

In the 1973–1974 season, the Flyers became the first of the six new expansion teams from 1967 to win a Stanley Cup. The Flyers then shocked the hockey world when they won a championship for a second time the very next season. The Flyers notched playoff appearances for the next 14 seasons in a row.

Along the way, the Flyers and their physical style have led to some intense rivalries. Historically, their biggest rival has been the New York Rangers. Their heated relationship stretches back to the 1970s. The Flyers also consider the New York Islanders, New Jersey Devils, and the Penguins among their chief rivals.

When the Flyers retired Mark Howe's number 2 in 2012, he became the fifth Flyer to have his jersey number retired in Philadelphia.

The Arena

The Wells Fargo Center has hosted many hockey related events. It recently hosted the 2010 Stanley Cup Final.

When Ed Snider was awarded an NHL franchise in Philly, he was required to immediately build an arena for his new team. Eleven months after its groundbreaking, the Philadelphia Spectrum was completed. It was at this arena that the Flyers made five of their eight Stanley Cup Final appearances. They played at the Spectrum for 29 seasons before moving to their new $210 million arena.

On October 5, 1996, the Flyers played their first regular season game at the Wells Fargo Center. It did not take long for the Flyers to adapt to their new home. The team became Eastern Conference Champions that year and reached the Stanley Cup Final. The move to the Wells Fargo Center has increased nightly attendance by more than 2,000 spectators.

In 2011, the Wells Fargo Center received an upgrade to its scoreboard. It now contains High-Definition and Light-Emission Diode (LED) technology to offer visitors a more memorable experience and a clearer picture of what is taking place on the ice. The arena also hosts concerts and family events.

The Flyers honored their two back-to-back Stanley Cup victories with a statue outside the Wells Fargo Center.

Where They Play

CANADA

British Columbia **7**

Alberta **4**

3

Saskatchewan

Manitoba **14**

Ontario

Washington

Montana

North Dakota

Minnesota **11**

Wisconsin

8

Oregon

Idaho

Wyoming

South Dakota

Iowa

Illinois

UNITED

Nevada

Utah

Colorado **9**

Nebraska

13

Missouri

6

STATES

California

5

1

Arizona **2**

New Mexico

Kansas

Oklahoma

Arkansas

Pacific Ocean

MEXICO

Texas **10**

Louisiana

Mississi

Gulf of Mexico

PACIFIC DIVISION

1	Anaheim Ducks	5	Los Angeles Kings
2	Arizona Coyotes	6	San Jose Sharks
3	Calgary Flames	7	Vancouver Canucks
4	Edmonton Oilers		

CENTRAL DIVISION

8	Chicago Blackhawks	12	Nashville Predators
9	Colorado Avalanche	13	St. Louis Blues
10	Dallas Stars	14	Winnipeg Jets
11	Minnesota Wild		

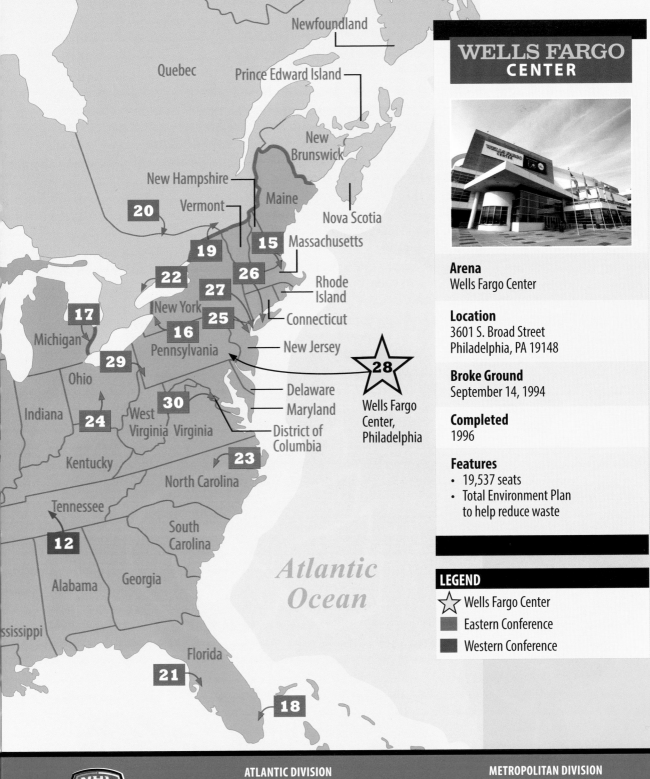

WELLS FARGO CENTER

Arena
Wells Fargo Center

Location
3601 S. Broad Street
Philadelphia, PA 19148

Broke Ground
September 14, 1994

Completed
1996

Features
- 19,537 seats
- Total Environment Plan to help reduce waste

LEGEND
☆ Wells Fargo Center
Eastern Conference
Western Conference

28 Wells Fargo Center, Philadelphia

ATLANTIC DIVISION

15	Boston Bruins	19	Montreal Canadiens
16	Buffalo Sabres	20	Ottawa Senators
17	Detroit Red Wings	21	Tampa Bay Lightning
18	Florida Panthers	22	Toronto Maple Leafs

METROPOLITAN DIVISION

23	Carolina Hurricanes	27	New York Rangers
24	Columbus Blue Jackets	☆ 28	Philadelphia Flyers
25	New Jersey Devils	29	Pittsburgh Penguins
26	New York Islanders	30	Washington Capitals

Philadelphia Flyers **11**

The Uniforms

The Flyers winged "P" design has remained unchanged since the team began play in **1967**.

The Flyers first wore the black jerseys as their alternative jersey. Later, they wore black when they played on the road. The black was then used as a home jersey. Finally, the team stopped wearing the black jerseys altogether in 2010.

HOME

There are some fans in Philadelphia today who watched the very first Flyers game in 1967. These fans can attest to the fact that the Flyers' jerseys have not changed very much through the years. The Flyers' jerseys have always been orange, black, and white. During the team's early years, players wore orange at home games and white at away games. In the 1970s and 1980s, the jersey colors for home and away games were reversed. In 2010, the team went back to wearing orange at home and white on the road.

AWAY

The center of each jersey features the Flyers **logo**, which is a black winged letter "P" that represents the city of Philadelphia. The P is bordered in white with an orange circle appearing in the middle.

In a 2008 *Hockey News* poll, the flying "P" logo ranked as the sixth best in the NHL.

Helmets and Face Masks

In 2002, the Flyers added their logo to the side of their helmets. Prior to that, the helmet only featured the word **FLYERS**.

Team captain Claude Giroux wears a helmet equipped with a protective visor. As a veteran NHL player, wearing a visor is optional for Giroux. Beginning in 2013, visors became mandatory for all new NHL players.

As with any contact sport, hockey requires protection to prevent injury. Numerous head injuries are reported in hockey each year, making helmets an absolute necessity. The Flyers always make sure to wear their helmets during each game. For their home games, they wear black helmets. On the road, they wear white head gear. Both home and away helmets have a decal of the team logo on each side, and a player's number on the front and back.

Goalie helmets are quite different. They are larger in order to protect the goalie's head, as well as his face, from incoming pucks. Since they are larger, goalies use the extra space to add personalized artwork. Current Flyers goalie Steve Mason wears a face mask decorated with zombie mock-ups of his teammates. Along the bottom front of his mask is Mason's nickname, "Mase." Mason's face mask is painted in the Flyers' colors and also displays the team's logo.

The tradition of goalies designing their face masks is alive and well in Philly today with Steve Mason, just as it was nearly 40 years ago with Wayne Stephenson.

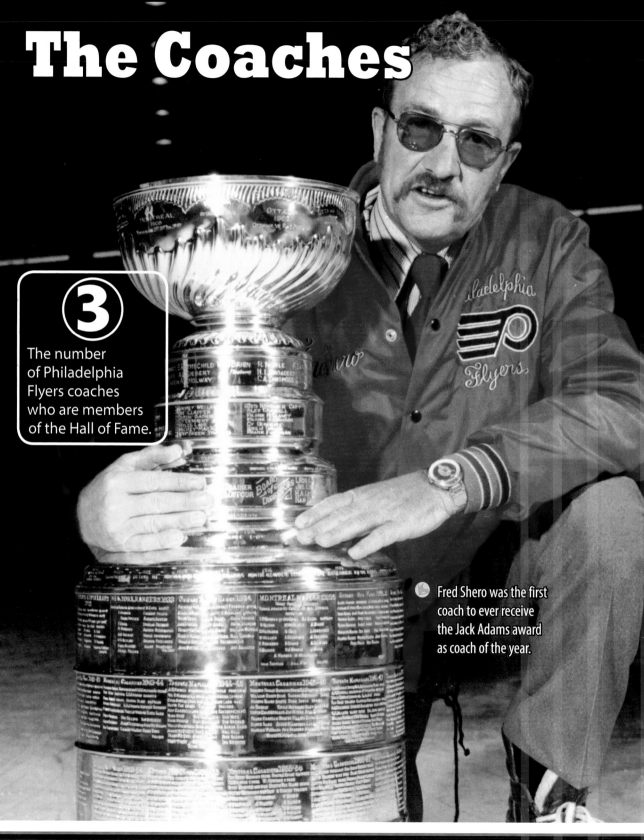

The Coaches

3

The number of Philadelphia Flyers coaches who are members of the Hall of Fame.

Fred Shero was the first coach to ever receive the Jack Adams award as coach of the year.

The Flyers have played 47 seasons in the NHL and only missed the postseason nine times. There have been a host of coaches who have overseen these winning teams. Over the years, five of these 18 coaches were awarded the Jack Adams Award as the Coach of the Year.

FRED SHERO In his younger days, Fred Shero was a boxing champion. He brought this fighting intensity and toughness to his role as leader of the Flyers. Shero directed the Flyers to their only two Stanley Cup championships in team history. He was later inducted into the Hockey Hall of Fame.

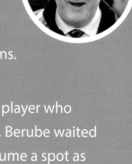

PAT QUINN Almost immediately after his NHL playing career ended, Pat Quinn assumed the head coaching job in Philadelphia. Quinn led the team to winning records in each of his four seasons and to a Stanley Cup Final appearance in 1980. After he left the team in 1991, he went on to coach four other NHL teams.

CRAIG BERUBE Craig Berube is another former player who returned to coach the Flyers. Unlike Pat Quinn, Berube waited 10 years after his playing career ended to assume a spot as the Flyers head coach. In his first season in 2013, Berube led Philadelphia to a 42–30–10 record, good for a third place finish in the Metropolitan Division. Berube's team reached the playoffs, though they were eliminated in the first round by the Rangers.

Fans and the Internet

PHILLE VILLE THRILLE!!

Flyers fans attend home games decked out in Flyers gear from head to toe, making the stands at the Wells Fargo Center look like a sea of orange.

Philadelphia fans are among the most loyal in all of sports. The Flyers have not won the Stanley Cup in 40 years, yet fans continue to brave the winter weather in Philadelphia to support their home team. When they are not in the Wells Fargo Center cheering on the Flyers, they are online sharing thoughts, photos, and videos about their team.

In addition to the official NHL Flyers website, fans follow their Flyers on a number of blogs. One popular blog is Broad Street Hockey, www.broadstreethockey,com, where fans can write their own articles and comment on other fans' write-ups. The website links to Twitter, so fans can easily access their profiles and reach out to other members of the Flyers community.

Signs
of a fan

#1 For the past 18 seasons, loyal Philadelphia fans have not allowed their average attendance to dip below 19,000.

#2 Fans show their spirit at each game. Some show up with face paint, orange hats, or even orange lycra body suits.

Legends of the Past

Many great players have suited up for the Broad Street Bullies. A few of them have become icons of the team and the city it represents.

Bobby Clarke

Bobby Clarke has only played and worked for one NHL organization, the Philadelphia Flyers. His 15-year playing career in Philadelphia was marked by both personal and team success. Clarke was a skilled offensive and defensive player, and was widely acknowledged as one of the best two-way forwards of all time. Clarke was the captain of the Flyers for 10 seasons. In two of those seasons, the Flyers won the Stanley Cup. Clarke currently serves as the Flyers' Senior Vice President.

Position: Center
NHL Seasons: 15 (1969–1984)
Born: August 13, 1949,
in Flin Flon, Manitoba, Canada

Bernie Parent

Hall of Fame goalie, Bernie Parent, did not learn how to skate until he was 11. Nine years later, he played in his first NHL game with the Boston Bruins. In 1967, he was acquired by the Flyers and went on to win two Stanley Cups in Philadelphia. In both of those championship seasons, Parent was awarded the Conn Smythe Trophy as the Most Valuable Player of the playoffs, as well as the Vezina Trophy as the league's best goaltender.

Position: Goalie
NHL Seasons: 14 (1965–1979)
Born: April 3, 1945, in Montreal, Quebec, Canada

Mark Howe

There were high expectations for Mark Howe, son of legendary hockey great, Gordie Howe. Mark lived up to those expectations with a Hall of Fame hockey career that spanned 16 NHL seasons and three different organizations. While in Philadelphia, his career took flight as he played in four **All-Star** games and was a three-time finalist for the James Norris Memorial Trophy, awarded to the NHL's top defenseman. Howe is currently the director of professional scouting for the Detroit Red Wings.

Position: Defenseman
NHL Seasons: 16 (1979–1995)
Born: May 28, 1955,
in Detroit, Michigan, United States

Bill Barber

Bill Barber is a Philadelphia Flyers' lifer. After playing all 12 of his NHL seasons for the Flyers, Barber has since returned to the organization. After a few seasons as the Flyers' head coach, he now serves as a scouting consultant for his beloved team. As part of the famous Leach, Clarke, Barber (LCB) **line**, Barber helped lead the Flyers to the franchise's only two Stanley Cups in 1974 and 1975. After an impressive eight seasons with the Flyers, he became their fifth team captain. Barber was inducted into the Hall of Fame in 1990.

Position: Left Wing
NHL Seasons: 12 (1972–1984)
Born: July 11, 1952,
in Callander, Ontario, Canada

Stars of Today

Today's Broad Street Bullies team is made up of many young, talented players who have proven that they are among the best in the league.

Claude Giroux

A goal scorer and offensive force of the highest caliber, Claude Giroux did not need much time to get used to the speed of hockey at the NHL level. In just his second season, he helped direct the Flyers to the Stanley Cup Final. While there, he netted a game-winning goal in game three against the Chicago Blackhawks. During the 2011–2012 season, he led the team with 65 assists. After five seasons with the Flyers, the two-time All-Star was recently named the team's 19th captain.

Position: Right Wing
NHL Seasons: 7 (2007–2014)
Born: January 12, 1988, in Hearst, Ontario, Canada

Jakub Voracek

Jakub Voracek joined the NHL from the Czech Republic when the Columbus Blue Jackets made him their first round pick in the 2007 NHL **Entry Draft**. After a short but impressive career in Columbus, he was traded to Philadelphia in 2011. Since joining the Flyers, Voracek's stats and play have improved steadily. In the 2013–2014 season, he reached several career-highs. In his 82 games that season, Voracek notched 23 goals and 39 assists for a total of 62 points. In 2012, Voracek signed a four-year contract extension to remain in Philadelphia.

Position: Right Wing
NHL Seasons: 6 (2008–2014)
Born: August 15, 1989, in Kladno, Central Bohemian Region, Czech Republic

Wayne Simmonds

Wayne Simmonds is a feisty competitor and a skilled scorer. After three seasons with the Los Angeles Kings, Simmonds was traded to the Flyers. In the 2013–2014 season, he took his offensive game to another level, scoring 29 times and adding in 31 **assists** for a total of 60 points. He plays the game with a ton of energy and always seems to be in the middle of things. Simmonds signed a four-year deal in 2012 to remain in Philadelphia through the 2015–2016 season.

Position: Right Wing
NHL Seasons: 6 (2008–2014)
Born: August 26, 1988, in Scarborough, Ontario, Canada

Sean Couturier

Before he joined the NHL, Sean Couturier played in the Quebec Major Junior Hockey League (QMJHL) with the Drummondville Voltigeurs. The QMJHL is one of Canada's three primary junior hockey leagues. Couturier was drafted by Philadelphia in the first round of the NHL Entry Draft in 2011. In his **rookie** season with the Flyers, he netted 13 goals, four of which were game-winners. He also added in 14 assists and continues to develop as a playmaker. Couturier was nominated for the Calder Memorial Trophy as the Rookie of the Year in the 2011–2012 season and remains a key player as the Flyers aim to return the Stanley Cup to the City of Brotherly Love.

Position: Center
NHL Seasons: 3 (2011–2014)
Born: December 7, 1992, in Phoenix, Arizona, United States

All-Time Records

60
Most Goals in a Single Season
During the 1975–1976 season, Reggie Leach set the franchise record for most goals in a single season with 61. He is the only player in franchise history with more than 60 goals in one season.

11,669
Most Saves Made
Ron Hextall played with the Flyers for 11 seasons. Hextall managed to make 11,669 saves during that span.

50
Most Shutouts
Bernie Parent recorded 12 shutouts during both the 1973–1974 and 1974–1975 seasons. While these are single-season franchise records, he also holds the franchise record with 50 career shutouts.

123

Most Points in a Single Season

During the 1992–1993 season, Mark Recchi recorded 123 points. Those 123 points set a Flyers' franchise record and a career high for Recchi.

61

Most Game-Winning Goals

In his 10 years with the Flyers, John LeClair played in 649 games and managed to set a franchise record with 61 game-winning goals.

Timeline

Throughout the team's history, the Philadelphia Flyers have had many memorable events that have become defining moments for the team and its fans.

1974
After six Stanley Cup Final games, the Flyers defeat the Boston Bruins and become champions for the first time.

1968
The Flyers appear in their first playoff game against the St. Louis Blues.

| 1960 | 1965 | 1970 | 1975 | 1980 | 1985 |

In 1966, Ed Snider, Bill Putnam, and Joe Scott pay $2 million to purchase an NHL franchise for Philadelphia.

1976
After reaching the Stanley Cup Final for their third season in a row, the Flyers are defeated by the Montreal Canadiens.

1975
The team wins its second Stanley Cup in a row, defeating the Buffalo Sabres 2–0 to clinch the series.

The Future

It has been 40 years since the Flyers have won the Stanley Cup. However, their continued playoff appearances—as well as Stanley Cup Final appearances—indicate a franchise that is poised for a Cup breakthrough. With young stars and veteran leadership sprinkled throughout the roster, the Flyers have the right mix of youth and experience to reward the patience of their longtime fans.

1988

Founder Ed Snider is elected to the Hall of Fame. He had been associated with the Flyers for 22 years.

In 2010, the Flyers advance to the Stanley Cup Final, but are defeated by the Chicago Blackhawks in six games.

1990 **1995** **2000** **2005** **2010** **2015**

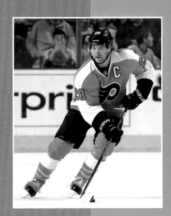

2014

Entering the 2014–2015 season, the Flyers have reached the playoffs in all but two seasons since 1994–1995.

1996

The team plays its first game at the Wells Fargo Center.

Write a Biography

Life Story

A person's life story can be the subject of a book. This kind of book is called a biography. Biographies often describe the lives of people who have achieved great success. These people may be alive today, or they may have lived many years ago. Reading a biography can help you learn more about a great person.

Get the Facts

Use this book, and research in the library and on the internet, to find out more about your favorite Flyer. Learn as much about this player as you can. What position does he play? What are his statistics in important categories? Has he set any records? Also, be sure to write down key events in the person's life. What was his childhood like? What has he accomplished off the field? Is there anything else that makes this person special or unusual?

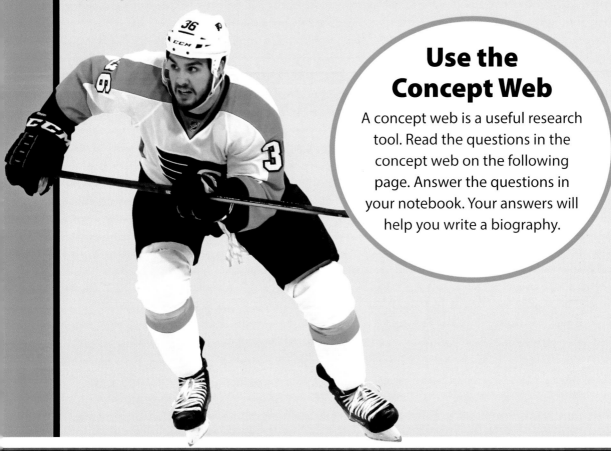

Use the Concept Web

A concept web is a useful research tool. Read the questions in the concept web on the following page. Answer the questions in your notebook. Your answers will help you write a biography.

Concept Web

Adulthood
- Where does this individual currently reside?
- Does he or she have a family?

Your Opinion
- What did you learn from the books you read in your research?
- Would you suggest these books to others?
- Was anything missing from these books?

Childhood
- Where and when was this person born?
- Describe his or her parents, siblings, and friends.
- Did this person grow up in unusual circumstances?

Accomplishments off the Field
- What is this person's life's work?
- Has he or she received awards or recognition for accomplishments?
- How have this person's accomplishments served others?

Write a Biography

Help and Obstacles
- Did this individual have a positive attitude?
- Did he or she receive help from others?
- Did this person have a mentor?
- Did this person face any hardships?
- If so, how were the hardships overcome?

Accomplishments on the Field
- What records does this person hold?
- What key games and plays have defined his career?
- What are his stats in categories important to his position?

Work and Preparation
- What was this person's education?
- What was his or her work experience?
- How does this person work?
- What is the process he or she uses?

Trivia Time

Take this quiz to test your knowledge of the Philadelphia Flyers. The answers are printed upside down under each question.

1 How many Stanley Cups have the Flyers won?

A. Two

2 Who played in the most games as a Flyer?

A. Bobby Clarke

3 Who is the Flyer's current coach?

A. Craig Berube

4 How much did the Flyers' owners pay for their Philadelphia franchise in 1967?

A. $2 million

5 What are the team's main colors?

A. Orange, white, and black

6 Which coach directed the Flyers to their two Stanley Cup victories?

A. Fred Shero

7 Which player is the team's current captain?

A. Claude Giroux

8 How many times have the Flyers reached the Stanley Cup Final?

A. Eight

9 Where does the team currently play?

A. The Wells Fargo Center

Key Words

All-Star: a game made for the best-ranked players in the NHL that happens mid-season. A player can be named an All-Star and then be sent to play in this game.

assists: a statistic that is attributed to up to two players of the scoring team who shoot, pass, or deflect the puck toward the scoring teammate

entry draft: an annual meeting where different teams in the NHL are allowed to pick new, young players who can join their teams

expansion: expansion in the NHL is marked by the addition of a new franchise. The league last expanded in 2000 when the Columbus Blue Jackets and Minnesota Wild joined the NHL.

franchise: a team that is a member of a professional sports league

line: forwards who play in a group, or "shift," during a game

logo: a symbol that stands for a team or organization

playoffs: a series of games that occur after regular season play

rookie: a player age 26 or younger who has played no more than 25 games in a previous season, nor six or more games in two previous seasons

shutout: a game in which the losing team is blocked from making any goals

Index

Log on to www.av2books.com

AV² by Weigl brings you media enhanced books that support active learning. Go to www.av2books.com, and enter the special code found on page 2 of this book. You will gain access to enriched and enhanced content that supplements and complements this book. Content includes video, audio, weblinks, quizzes, a slide show, and activities.

AV² Online Navigation

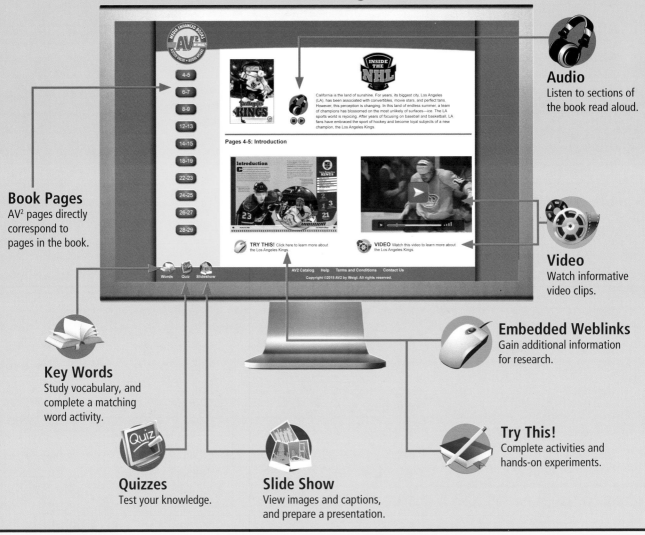

Audio
Listen to sections of the book read aloud.

Book Pages
AV² pages directly correspond to pages in the book.

Video
Watch informative video clips.

Embedded Weblinks
Gain additional information for research.

Key Words
Study vocabulary, and complete a matching word activity.

Try This!
Complete activities and hands-on experiments.

Quizzes
Test your knowledge.

Slide Show
View images and captions, and prepare a presentation.

AV² was built to bridge the gap between print and digital. We encourage you to tell us what you like and what you want to see in the future.

Sign up to be an AV² Ambassador at www.av2books.com/ambassador.